Dear Gerry,

May the Spirit fill you as you open your heart in prayer.

Ten Thoughts

on

Personal Prayer

by

Charles R Demers, PhD

Published November, 2015
ISBN 978-1518898273

Table of Contents

Why should I pray? 1

When should I pray? 9

Where should I pray? 13

How often should I pray? 17

How should I pray? 23

What prayer form works best for ME? 29

DOES God hear my prayers? 31

How do I know God hears my prayers? 33

When should I expect an answer to my prayers? 37

Will God love me more if I pray more? 39

Introduction

Over the years I have had many conversations about prayer.

Most of the conversations I have shared with my fellow Catholics. However, a fair number of chats have come up with other Christians, some Jews, door-to-door evangelizers, a sizeable number of non-believers, and others whose faith I did not know. No faith practice, no religion has an exclusive license on the perfect form of personal prayer.

In the course of the conversations we sometimes covered questions we had in our own faith lives. We have all struggled with it. We have all hungered for more. Some questions seem to arise repeatedly in many conversations about prayer.

Reflecting on the discussions and questions about prayer, without attribution to particular individuals or denominations, gave me a delightful sense that many people may want to share and consider what makes "good prayer." The disciples of Jesus Christ even asked Him **"Lord, teach us to pray just as John taught his disciples."** *(Luke 11:1)*

Making no pretense of any comparison between myself and Jesus, nor to any rabbinical talent of my own, I simply want to share the questions and my thoughts about them on personal prayer. My hope leads me to believe that some who read what I have written may accept, enjoy, and grow more comfortable with their personal prayer, may grow in their own prayer, and may come to a joyful personal prayer relationship with God. Take these thoughts not as answers to the questions, but as a stimulus to your own reflections.

The ten thoughts I have assembled fall into the classic "Who – what - when – where – how – why" categories. I suggest you also make this short book your beginning journal on personal prayer. As you read, make notes in the margin or in a journal you keep as a companion to this book.

Also, try starting your reading time with a brief moment of silence. Then, briefly, sincerely, and lovingly open your mind and heart, asking God to join your personal prayer, to enlighten you in your faith journey, and to help you transcend your human limitations to **"be perfect, just as your heavenly Father is perfect."** *(Matthew 5:48)* Make notes in your journal regarding any changes you may sense in your prayer. Finally, remember that personal prayer, like life itself, has bright days and stormy days, rich, full days and dry, barren days. Enjoy the wonder of each day's prayer and where it leads.

Gratitude

Thanks be to God and to all my friends and family who allowed God to work through them in helping me in developing, preparing, reviewing, and completing this guide to simple prayer.

Why should I pray?

"Pray as though everything depended on God.
Work as though everything depended on you."
~ Augustine of Hippo

Think for a moment about the times you pray; the situations in which you prayed in the past. You probably prayed as a child with your mother or father, just learning the basic prayers they wished to share with you. So, you experienced prayer as a sharing moment, a bonding time. We might think of this as prayer of communing or communion. Then as you made your way through school, no doubt you prayed for help in preparation for a big test or to help you play well in a sport or to make things better between you and a friend who had a difference of opinion. We call this prayer a form of petition.

As you grew older you may have known someone who fell sick or experienced some sad times. When you prayed for their benefit, you used intercessory prayer. If you did your brother or friend or someone harm, besides begging them to forgive you, you probably also prayed to God for forgiveness, knowing that when you hurt God's children, God's creation, you also hurt God. Other terms describing this type of prayer include contrition, reconciliation, or penance.

At any age, but certainly when your motives and your love is most sincere and pure, and you come to your prayer with a humble, open, and vulnerable standing, this reflects your <u>adoration</u> of God.

Though you may have read about many varieties or types of prayer in many other learned writings, the types above include the common categories.

So, why do you use any of them at all? Well, something deep inside you, something beyond the teachings of your parents, clergy, educators, spiritual directors, etc. may have taught you in your formative years and learning opportunities. You came to know **your** prayer in a natural sense. Jesus told His disciples as He neared His Passion and death that He would send His ***"Advocate to be with you always, the Spirit of truth, which the world cannot accept, because it neither sees nor knows it. But you know it, because it remains with you, and will be in you."*** *(John 14:16-17)* And Jesus added, ***"The Advocate, the holy Spirit that the Father will send in my name—he will teach you everything."*** *(John 14:26)*

We benefit today from what the disciples received after a period of waiting. The Advocate sent from God initiates our prayer.

As humans, every one of us also has a natural inclination to want interaction with others. We want to communicate our thoughts, our desires, our victories, our needs, our love, and our desire for others to love us. We NEED to communicate as a natural part of living.

Combine the initiation of spiritual life from God with our need to communicate with other intelligent beings and you have – prayer. Simply put, prayer is communication with God.

Now, many people forget or overlook the fact that communication involves not only talking (sharing our thoughts and ideas with others), but listening as well (hearing and understanding the thoughts and ideas others share with us). This happens at all levels of communications, including conversations between us mortals and our prayer with God.

WHY should we pray? Let us consider how it compares with our other human needs, including interpersonal communication. We have basic needs such as air, food and water, clothing and shelter. Without those we could not survive very long at all. Then we have secondary needs like sources of warmth, opportunities for socializing, tools for various tasks, transportation to move between societies and exchange goods, etc. As you can tell, I have grossly generalized the human needs. My intent is that we focus our attention on another fundamental human need - the need to communicate.

Every one of us has an innate drive to share our thoughts and desires with other people, and to hear the thoughts and desires of others. Life in total isolation from other intelligent beings may well drive some of us mad.

Relative to our desire to communicate with people we naturally want and need to communicate with our God, the source of life and perfection, if only to try to discover the secret to life's perfection. We cannot NOT communicate with God. We cannot NOT pray.

We want to know the will of God. What does God want of us? What does God expect of us? To find out, we need to go to the Source; we need to ask God directly. To uncover or learn this important element of our lives we need to sit quietly and listen to God. We can learn God's will for us by choosing this better way, as Martha's sister Mary did (Lk. 10:42).

You may find that your prayer comes to you in the Holy Spirit in a unique and profound way that God intends ONLY for you. Rejoice in that gift. Bask in its radiance. Grow in the grace that you receive. However God gives you the gift of prayer, welcome it.

Wait Patiently for God.

> ***"Be still before the LORD; wait for God."***
> *(Psalms 37:7)*

In our prayer, many of us eagerly grasp to possess our God. We want to hold Him and never let Him go. However, scripture tells us that we do not so much possess God; rather God comes to take hold of us. Though our words do not say so directly, we often tell God, "I need You to do this (for me or for someone else). Now, God, go do as I have told You."

In spite of our good intentions, we don't wait and listen for God to tell us what we need to do. Even when we do discern what God wants of us, we don't drop whatever we have started doing to rush off to do what God asks of us. Instead, we tell God what we have decided God should do. Similarly, when we discern God's will for us, we tend to "adjust" God's will to better fit our own will.

So, we may negotiate with God. We may try to persuade God. We may even compromise with God on what we do in response to God's will. We do NOT listen to God and act on what God tells us. We do not pray, and then work on what God has asked of us in prayer.

We pray more like the Pharisee than the tax collector (Luke 18:9-14). "The Pharisee took up his position and spoke this prayer to himself." The Pharisee does not open himself vulnerably and direct his prayer to God. Rather, he speaks his prayer about himself and his own qualifications and achievements.

We pray for many reasons. However, one fundamental reason for our prayer involves opening ourselves to God's will and call to our heart. Prayer can and does change us. It raises our awareness of God's forgiveness toward us. In turn, our prayer tends to turn our heart toward forgiveness and compassion towards others in their challenges. Prayer can allow us to find God in our neighbor. The Pharisee misses this point as he speaks "this prayer to himself." The tax collector, on the other hand, knows very well that he needs God's help and begs for forgiveness. He focuses on God and God's mercy, not on himself.

We do not pray for ourselves. We think we pray for ourselves and for others. In fact, though we may intercede for the benefit of others, our prayer ultimately centers on our gaining awareness of God's will and accepting it; surrender to the will of God. We do what God has told us He wants and needs because He loves us, in spite of our faults and failings.

In prayer we pay attention to God's presence. We move

closer to God's presence. We hunger for God's presence. Finally, like the lost sheep, we accept God's presence, and, with God's gift of grace, do our best to live with the tension of God's presence. While we live our mortal lives we live tensely and tentatively with God's presence.

Most of us find real prayer truly difficult. We cannot see God or touch God or hear God, as we do with other human beings with whom we communicate. God tests our faith. In doing so, God builds our faith, or we run from it and destroy it.

Most of us experience great difficulty finding God, especially in the privacy of our prayer. We do not know how to let God find us. In the depths of our being we know the Father as the source of our very life, our whole being. Every breath we take, every act of every day, no matter how insignificant, draws us toward the Divine, hungers for it, desires envelopment by it. Though we rarely, if ever, realize it, we really want to surrender and let God possess us.

In true prayer, God initiates. Our prayer, then, always responds to God's invitation. To respond, we must first listen attentively to the Holy Spirit alive within us. So, prayer actually arises as response to God rather than a call from us to God.

God exists in our human or worldly sense in sublime rather than overt or tangible ways. We must heighten our awareness to that elusive, fragile, and easily missed presence. We will struggle with our awareness, so we need to persevere and persist. When we find God, we will realize that we have finally allowed God to find us.

We have allowed the prayer of the Spirit who lives in us to pray in silence, "Abba, Father!"

We pray, then, to begin to tear down our self-reflecting mirrors and allow God to move just a fraction of a measure closer to us.

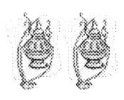

When should I pray?

"Courage is fear that has said its prayers."
~ Dorothy Bernard

Every living, breathing minute of your life -- anything less would leave you unsatisfied, that you had left yourself before God without presenting your whole case. Yes, prayer can sometimes seem like presenting a court case before the Highest Court. You need to represent your spirit with the best you can offer. If you have questions, ask. If you have objections, shout them out. If you have a point to make, make it known. If you think your spirit has less than a perfect record... accept it as true – God knows everything; ask for mercy. If you need help or clarification, demand it.

When you fail to see God, do what you must to find God again. Whenever you have put up a barrier between yourself and God, get rid of it. God loves you. God has the power to judge. God shows mercy. God can punish. God is love. Love. Love in its warmest, calmest, deepest, most powerful sense.

God always wants you; wants the best for you. Ask God questions from your heart. Tell God your thoughts. Chat with God. Just BE with God. Sit with God and bask in the glow. Enjoy what God offers.

WHEN do you do this? Constantly. When you wake. When you go to sleep. When you eat. When you breathe. When you have a crisis. When you have a victory. When you have a challenge. When you have a need. When you love someone. When you hate someone. When you want to talk to someone. When you don't want to talk to anyone. When you reach a happy point. When you fall into sadness. When you hunger for food or drink or love or attention or respect. When you don't. When you have a home to shelter you. When you have lost your home. When you have the finest clothes. When your clothes seem to be threadbare holes held together by a few patches. When they have a parade down Main Street in your honor. When they ignore you and leave you forgotten. Pray. Never stop praying.

Can we say more or less about when to pray?

In our human existence we develop patterns of when to pray. As children, we learn to pray at bedtime. As we become students, the moments before a test launch us into desperate prayer. Later, as adults, we pray when we need something like a mortgage payment or when we get lost or if we need to find a new job. We often offer intercessory prayer for friends or family members who fall seriously ill. In other words, we tend to pray when we want something from God. God accepts our prayers and answers them. We may not like God's answer, but God does answer our prayers, no matter how mundane.

We do need to have patterns in our daily lives, however. We get up, bathe, dress, eat breakfast, etc. If we establish habitual times and forms of prayer, we incorporate prayer as a part of our lives. For example, we might pray in the morning after we dress. This brief pause sets a tone for our day and a focus for our lives. We might establish a habit of praying silently before each meal, or audibly with family members, let us say, before the evening meal. Then, we can close our day, just before climbing into bed, with reflections on our day, prayers of thanks or petitions for emotional strength, etc. Your own ideas can add or modify this brief list to fit your own life's needs. Of course you can adjust your prayer patterns even long after you have established them, based on changes in your life, and according to evolving spiritual needs.

Few of us have maintained a practice of sacramental Reconciliation or even expressing our sorrow for having hurt God. Rarely do we pray in thanks to God. Pray for help with important decisions. Some of us have never simply sat in God's presence to simply adore.

God deserves more. Don't hold back.

Set yourself some particular times to pray. Morning prayer. Evening Prayer. Night prayer. Prayers at meals. Then mark your life with other events at which you will share your life with God. Victories, losses, pains, pleasures... you decide. Pick a handful and write them in your personal calendar or make a mental note of them. Remind yourself of them. Pray. Pray. Pray.

In between, don't forget to listen. If you expect God to listen, don't forget to listen to God. God appreciates when you listen to His replies, to his admonitions, to His counsel, to His loving words. Listening is the other part of prayer, maybe the more important part.

Practice your listening skills. Make time in the morning, before breakfast, or in the evening before dinner, or both. Go to a quiet corner in your home and just listen for about 20 minutes. Listen for God in the beating of your heart and the rhythm of your breathing. More on this in the following chapters.

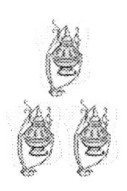

Where should I pray?

*"We may explore the universe and find ourselves,
or we may explore ourselves and find the universe.
It matters not which of these paths we choose."
~ Diana Robinson*

Of course, every one of us should "pray at every opportunity." (*Ephesians 6:18*). Therefore, if we pray at every opportunity, we pray at every location where we find ourselves. We pray everywhere.

A structure focused on faith does not, in itself, sanctify the place (See other authors for the related topic of Real Presence in the Eucharist); our prayer makes a place of faith. To paraphrase a bumper-sticker expression, "Standing in a garage no more makes you a car than standing in a church makes you a person of faith."

In praying everywhere we make our every-day activities a form of prayer. We make eating meals prayer. We make our personal cleansing prayer. We make our work prayer. We even make our play a prayer. As prayer, our every action, word, and thought we consecrate and offer to our God. If so, then we remain always in our prayer sanctuary. In another view, as many learned theologians have put it, our sanctuary remains within us. On our faith journey, we have our prayer sanctuary constantly within ourselves. In this sanctuary, we offer God a home within us. At every moment, we should assure God of a clean and warm place to stay. THIS is prayer.

Still, let us concern ourselves with the prayer in which we focus every fiber of our being on communicating with God. What we traditionally think of as prayer does have a special meaning for us as human beings. We focus ourselves, at certain times of the day or at special moments, in communication with our Creator, our Savior, to adore, to listen, to petition, to confess, to question, and sometimes, just to BE with our God.

Typically, many of us start and end our day with some form of prayer. If we think of our prayer as a special conversation with someone we respect, we would do that in a place set apart. To make this a special and most respectful communication, we should arrange our home prayer place as a "place apart," with at least a minimal altar. This can mean, quite simply, something to remind us of our God, such as a crucifix, an icon, a Bible on a small table or top of a dresser. In a humble home, your altar, your prayer sanctuary may simply be a chair near a crucifix or icon on the wall.

In many ways, the simpler your place of prayer the better. First, simplicity helps keep costs low. Second, commonality keeps your space available for the rest of your family or for other, normal home and family needs. Third, using standard room layouts and ordinary furniture minimizes disruption of your prayer space. (NOTE: Presence of a crucifix, icon, and or Bible, however, will sometimes initiate an "evangelization opportunity.") If you have been blessed with more or larger rooms, consider it an opportunity to occasionally share your home with those who have less.

Having a Bible in our place of prayer always helps. We may begin with a brief reading. We can refer to a Bible passage that arises in our meditation. We can read scripture passages, dividing our readings with several minutes of reflective meditation. We might even close our prayer time with a short scripture. Whatever helps makes your place of prayer a special place of respect for God in your daily life makes it your sanctuary.

Designate one or more times during your day for prayer. At the same time (or times) of every day, retreat to your prayer sanctuary and spend time in prayer with God, just as you do with the very special people in your life. Close out other distractions of your daily life for this brief prayer time. Focus on God alone at this time. When possible, pray at the same time(s) each day. This, along with your "place apart," will not only help you to make this a habit, but will also help others learn to respect your prayer time and place.

When traveling, or on days when you cannot pray in your home sanctuary or at your customary prayer time, think about when and/or where you will make time for prayer. God understands that our lives do not stand still. So, reserve some small place and specific time for each day during your travels. This helps you maintain your prayer habit as closely to your normal routine as possible.

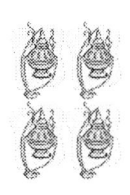

How often should I pray?

"To be a Christian without prayer is no more possible than to be alive without breathing."
~ Martin Luther King Jr.

Most of us eat three meals each day, plus a snack or two, just to maintain ourselves. We shower or bathe once, sometimes twice daily, not to mention the frequent hand washings to keep our bodies hygienic. Following the guidance of dentists, we also brush twice each day, maybe more. Most of us do some reading every day, whether from books, newspapers, magazines, or the Internet. That doesn't even count food package labels, clothing labels, billboards, road signs, printed material on TV, or other incidental reading.

So, you get the idea that we do many things on a daily basis to maintain or improve ourselves as human beings. We do these for our physical, intellectual, social, or cultural well-being. We also have an innate hunger for spiritual maintenance and betterment. To do that, we pray daily.

Daily prayer helps maintain good spiritual health in much the same way that good nutrition helps maintain good physical health.

What would happen to our physical well-being if we ate only at Christmas, Easter, weddings, and funerals? We might eventually die of starvation. Similarly, if we stopped reading, our intellectual capabilities would begin to suffer more and more as we read less and less. Reduced bathing and dental care would not only cause some physical deterioration, but would make us socially and culturally handicapped as well.

Prayer reduction or elimination has the same effect on our spiritual lives.

How much prayer do we need to maintain a good spiritual life? At what level or frequency of prayer does our spiritual health diminish? At what prayer level does spiritual growth occur in each of us?

Unfortunately, I have no clear answers for you. However, let us talk about cause and effect for a minute. The cause of reduced food intake would likely have the effect of health problems. How much? Well, that varies with each person. Reduced reading would eventually have the effect of diminished intellect. How soon? How great? That, also, varies with each individual. Prayer increase and decrease will also have a unique effect on your spiritual health.

Let us begin with some basics, then increase or reduce them to see how it affects you.

We can begin by opening our day with a morning prayer to set the tone of our spiritual connection with God. A greeting, some praise or adoration, a few requests for help or health complete our morning prayer chat with God. At bedtime, we give thanks, ask forgiveness for our acts of poor judgment and ill-chosen words, and ask for protection for our loved ones and ourselves. Maybe we stop briefly in our day to ask God for help, express our contrition for acting or speaking poorly, or share our wonder with God over some incredibly beautiful (or frightening) aspect of creation. That makes up the prayer life of most modern humans, at least in Anglo America.

What if we increased our daily prayer in some way? What if we diminished our daily prayer in some way? Let's explore that a bit.

Most of us do some sort of physical exercise. In fact, everyone probably does several kinds of exercise. We walk. We might ride a bike. We might run. We might play ball. Some of us swim. Some skate. Lots of people hike. Our physical exercise has favorites and variety. Just because we walk doesn't mean we wouldn't get pleasure out of going for a hike now and then. On top of that, we might enjoy swimming, too.

The same holds true for prayer. Some people start with praying with the Church community on Sunday, plus a few simple prayers each morning and bedtime. Some friends now invite you to visit their charismatic prayer group. Should you go? Why not? You read a magazine article about Centering Prayer. It inspires you to look more deeply into that prayer practice. A family member gets very sick or dies. You spend more time in intercessory prayer for that person.

Sometimes you lose interest in a particular form of prayer. Other times, your schedule changes and you need to adjust your prayer to fit your life changes. You may enjoy the musical prayer of singing in your Church choir. Then, you move to a new area and the choir membership works differently than in your former Church. The new choir doesn't quite suit your musical prayer needs. Or the meditation time you preferred now gets interrupted by your caring for a sick friend. Instead, you spend some time sharing spiritual reading with your friend.

Adding to your current prayer life or changing your prayer life doesn't hurt it. If anything, it re-energizes it, adds new life to it. Changes to your prayer habits often result from the breath of the Holy Spirit within you, calling you in new and greater directions. Listen to your inner spirit. Discuss it with God. Discern where God calls you to go. Then take the leap in prayer.

At the very least, start and end your days with prayer. Wake up to a brief chat with God, asking for blessings on your thoughts, words, and actions of the coming day. Thank God for the gift of this new day and all it holds. Take some time to sit and listen to God, preferably after reading briefly from scripture. Reflect or meditate on that scripture and listen for where God wants to take you today.   Then, once you have God's blessing, start your day on the right foot. Stay open to God to reach you all through the day.

At bedtime, reflect on where you met God through the day. More importantly, think about where you diverted your day away from God. Chat with God about how that happened. Reflect on how you can keep from falling down in that fashion tomorrow. Then, ask for God's forgiveness and mercy. Finally, ask for God's blessing and grace to end your day. Then sleep in peace.

If you have never tried praying with a group or congregation of people, you owe it to yourself to try praying with others. In fact, try several different forms of group prayer. For example, you might pray with a traditional group in a scheduled prayer service for several occasions. Also, spend a few sessions with a charismatic group. Take the opportunity to participate in prayer with a musical or singing group in prayer, such as your church choir or another less formal musical prayer group. Don't forget to experience a silent prayer group for several sessions. A nearby monastery should have one or more existing silent prayer groups.

You will find that the experience of praying with other people differs from praying alone in surprising ways that only God can explain. Even praying silently with others has a dynamic of the Spirit that will affect you in a profound sense. Of course, the music of a choir, the movement of charismatic prayer, and the rhythm of other forms of prayer will also have unique impacts on your spirit as well. Make the effort; reap the rewards.

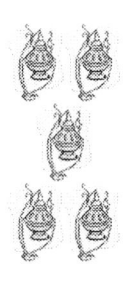

How should I pray?

It is better in prayer to have a heart without words than words without a heart."
~ Mohandas Gandhi

Every one of us prays. We pray for good health or success in a test. We pray for friends or family. We pray for forgiveness and blessing. We pray in thanks. We also pray in adoration and praise of our God.

Do we pray sincerely? Sincere prayer means communicating with God; direct communication. A speaker sends a message to a listener. The listener receives the message – sometimes. In the communication of prayer, we often envision ourselves as the speaker, sending a message to God. God listens. When God speaks to us, we listen for God's message very rarely. So, for the majority of us, what we like to call prayer really means a monologue directed toward God.

So, how do we change this non-communication with God; this half-prayer?

Listen. This completes the communication with God.

Listen.

Listen to God in scripture reading. Listen to God in the Eucharist, the living scripture. Listen to God to complete your prayer.

Listen.

God speaks best in the language of silence. However, we humans need words. Words limit our understanding of God. When it comes to communicating with God, "*the Spirit comes to the aid of our weakness; for we do not know how to pray as we ought, but the Spirit itself intercedes with inexpressible groanings.*" (Romans 8:26)

To begin our journey in this prayer life of listening, we can practice **Lectio Divina**.

Although we have had the term **Lectio Divina** (*Divine Reading*) for nearly as long as we have had our Catholic Church, few have even heard the term before.

In the simplest form of *Lectio Divina* a reader chooses one or more verses of scripture, reads them, and reflects on them. This approach to *Lectio Divina* undoubtedly has spiritual benefit. Many centuries of practice have shown that the early monks developed a *Lectio Divina* prayer style as a prayer habit.

The early Church Fathers, especially St. Benedict, followed a four step *Lectio Divina* formula of *Lectio*

(Reading), *Meditatio* (Meditation), *Oratio* (Prayer), *Contemplatio* (Contemplation). Later, some included as many as three optional steps, which I include below.

Statio (Optional) – **Select a place for your Divine Reading.** Make it as quiet as possible, with minimal distraction. Closing doors or curtains may help. You may wish to have a candle. A silent timer with a soft-sounding bell can help you remain focused on God without thinking of the time. Choose a cushion or seat that allows you to keep your back straight and not uncomfortable. You want neither discomfort to distract your prayer, nor excess relaxation to make you fall asleep. Choose a mantra – a sacred word. You will use this word in your contemplative prayer. You will repeat it silently in your mind. Your mantra serves not as a point on which to focus; quite the opposite. Repeating it serves as a "mental broom" to clear your mind, allowing God to fill you with His will for you.

Lectio – **Reading and listening to the Word of God.** Open your heart to the Holy Spirit's guidance. Choose a brief scripture, preferably one or two verses from daily scripture or the scriptures of the coming Sunday. Read the scripture verse three times, with brief pauses between readings. In groups, one person reads aloud. Imagine that God has sent this scripture verse especially for you. Envision <u>your role</u> in the will of God in this scripture. Focus on God's overwhelming love for you as an individual. (5 minutes)

Meditatio – **Reflecting on the Word.** Read the scripture verse again, once. Let the Holy Spirit draw your attention to a particular word or short phrase within this scripture verse and what it means for you today. Remember that you have a unique relationship with God, so this word will also have unique meaning for you. (5 minutes)

Oratio – **The Prayer of the Heart.** Read the scripture verse one last time. Keep your heart open to the Holy Spirit working in you and through you. Put your voice at the disposal of the Holy Spirit. Keep in mind that God may use you as prophet to counsel or evangelize someone else. The words come from God in the Holy Spirit using your voice. In groups, share the prayer that the Holy Spirit has placed in your heart; no more than a sentence or two. If alone, remain open to God's prompting your prayer at some later time. Do not be afraid. (5 minutes)

Contemplatio – **Entering the silence "Too Deep for Words."** Now let the words go. As beautiful as we find the words of God in scripture, God speaks to us best in the language of silence. Relax your body. Energize your mind and your spirit. Slow your breathing. Let the Holy Spirit pray within you without words. As John the Baptist said, "He must increase; I must decrease." (John 3:30) Use your mantra, your sacred word. Repeat it silently in your mind. (20 minutes)

Collatio (Optional) – **Discussion.** In group sessions of *Lectio Divina*, we may choose to discuss and share our personal experiences.

Actio (Optional) – **Action.** Take the message God has placed in your heart and **live it**.

To find out more about **Lectio Divina**, find one of the many books on the subject in a Catholic book store.

Thomas Merton has written on the topic, as have Basil Pennington and Michael Casey, all Trappist monks. You may also wish to search for a periodic *Lectio Divina* e-mail reminder.

But if you *live* your prayer, then everything you **do**, everything you **say**, everything you **think** exists as prayer. When that happens, you will not think about "how" you pray. It will simply happen. Think for a moment about a simple question many adolescents ask of their parents – "When will I know I am in love?" And the classic parental reply: "When you find real love, you will know it."

AM I PRAYING RIGHT?[1]
"On that day you will ask in My name."
(John 16:26)

> Jesus promised: "I give you My assurance, whatever you ask the Father, He will give you in My name" (John 16:23). Jesus said: "I give you My word, if you are ready to believe that you will receive whatever you ask for in prayer, it shall be done for you" (Mark 11:24). He also promised: "I solemnly assure you, the man who has faith in Me will do the works I do, and greater far than these. Why? Because I go to the Father, and whatever you ask in My name I will do" (John 14:12-13). Jesus commands: "Ask and you shall receive, that your joy may be full" (John 16:24).

---

[1] This selection taken from "One Bread, One Body" (Saturday, 19May12), a publication of Presentation Ministries, Cincinnati, Ohio.

Do you get the impression we don't know how to pray as we ought, that our prayers are merely a shadow of what they could be? If we are to pray as the Lord means for us to pray, we need to pray in the Spirit (see Jude 20). The Spirit "helps us in our weakness, for we do not know how to pray as we ought" (Romans 8:26). Until "the Spirit Himself makes intercession for us" (Romans 8:26), we aren't praying by God's standards and much of the Biblical teaching on prayer seems farfetched.

Finally, let us close with a thought from a homily on prayer by Fr. Gene Pistacchio, OFM, preached at St. Anthony's Shrine, Arch Street, Boston.

"Prayer is like a power cord. It connects us with the greatest power in existence."

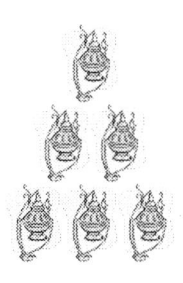

What prayer form works best for ME?

"What seem our worst prayers may really be, in God's eyes, our best. Those, I mean, which are least supported by devotional feeling. For these may come from a deeper level than feeling. God sometimes seems to speak to us most intimately when he catches us, as it were, off our guard."
~ C.S. Lewis

Interesting question...

Over the years you have undoubtedly tried numerous forms of prayer. Some worked well for you as a child. Then as you grew and matured, you searched for a prayer form or style that better suited the faith level in which you now felt more comfortable. Throughout your life these changes may have occurred many times. They likely will change as your needs change in the future.

Lots of choices, options; each occurring situationally or conditionally.

In times of celebration, in times of sorrow, in times of

doubt, and many other situations, you called on God in unique and different ways. God heard and responded to all of your prayers. Look deeply into your heart and ponder, or leap out with your prayer in joy or anger or pleading or contrition or sorrow, as the moment calls you. Ask a question of God, or tell Him your thoughts or simply ponder the depths of Wisdom or Love or Being. God does not reject, but lovingly embraces your every attempt to touch the Divine again and again.

YOU...and God... hold the answer.

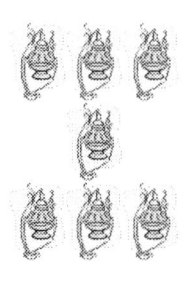

DOES God hear my prayers?

"Pray, and let God worry"
~ Martin Luther

Look around you. You see the condition of people of faith and those seriously lacking in faith. One seems no different than another. Poor people, wealthy people, people of one color or another, people in cities, people in wilderness areas, and everyone in between. Whose prayers does God answer? The textbook answer says God answers ALL prayers. We also know that God answers prayers in His way, in His time.

> **For as the heavens are higher than the earth,**
> **so are my ways higher than your ways,**
> **my thoughts higher than your thoughts.**
> *(Isaiah 55:9)*

also...

> **"With the Lord one day is like a thousand years**
> **and a thousand years like one day."**
> *(2 Peter 3:8)*

Pay close attention to your prayer requests and those of your faith friends.

Listen to God answering even your unspoken prayers. When you reflect and recognize that God has answered your prayers, first, express your sincere gratitude to God, then spend a brief time pondering whether you even expressed the answered prayer to God outwardly. When you realize that God has answered your unexpressed need, then you will know just how much God loves you, as an individual; cares for you by name, every moment of every day.

God hears you. Remember to take time to listen to God.

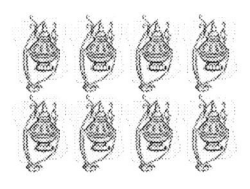

How do I know God hears my prayers?

"I know God will not give me anything I can't handle. I just wish He didn't trust me so much."
~ Mother Theresa of Calcutta

God tells us He hears our prayers. In fact, He tells us He anticipates our needs before we can begin to form a prayer in our hearts and minds.

> ***The LORD has eyes for the just***
> ***and ears for their cry.***
>
> ***When the just cry out, the LORD hears***
> ***and rescues them from all distress.***
>
> ***The LORD is close to the brokenhearted,***
> ***saves those whose spirit is crushed.***
>
> ***Many are the troubles of the just,***
> ***but the LORD delivers them from them all.***
>
> ***God watches over all their bones;***
> ***not one of them shall be broken.***

> *The LORD redeems his loyal servants;*
>> *God condemns none who take refuge in him.*
>> (Psalms 34:16, 18-21, 23)

Look (listen, feel) for God's reply.

> *"The coming of the kingdom of God cannot be observed... no one will announce, 'Look, here it is,' or, 'There it is.' For behold, the kingdom of God is among you."*
>> (Luke 17:20-21)

> *"Speak, for your servant is listening."*
>> (1 Samuel 3:10)

> *This is how we shall know that we belong to the truth and reassure our hearts before him in whatever our hearts condemn, for God is greater than our hearts and knows everything. Beloved, if [our] hearts do not condemn us, we have confidence in God and receive from him whatever we ask, because we keep his commandments and do what pleases him. And his commandment is this: we should believe in the name of his Son, Jesus Christ, and love one another just as he commanded us.*
>> (1 John 3:19:23)

Listen with your heart; connect to God with your heart. Then you will know God hears and answers not only your expressed prayers but all your needs.

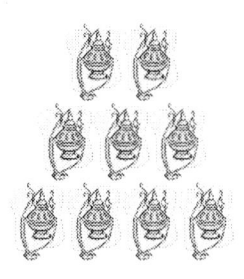

When should I expect an answer to my prayers?

"When the solution is simple, God is answering."
~ Albert Einstein

Patience. In our catechetical learning we Christians spent time learning the fruits of the Spirit (Galatians 5:22-23), including patience. If we live our Christianity fully and richly, we will do so with patience. We will know we have needs. We also know that others we love have needs. For these we pray in earnest. God hears us and answers our prayers in accord with His will for us.

God's time is not our time; our knowledge falls short of God's knowledge (Isaiah 55:6-11, Psalms 103:15-17). Without Divine knowledge we can never know all. God has no such limitation. Therefore, when we ask something of God in prayer, God takes our prayerful request and tempers it with the knowledge of Divine Wisdom.

In other words, if what we have asked in our prayer has goodness and merit, God grants and answers our prayer with any supplemental gifts necessary. If we have prayed for enlightenment and wisdom before making our request, we will little notice any Divine "adjustment" to our prayer request.

In our haste we sometimes listen to God less than we should. Then God answers our prayer requests with loving adjustments in quality, timing, or other refinements necessary for our growth and conversion.

When God determines that you need the answer, you will receive the answer to your prayer in all its richness and abundance.

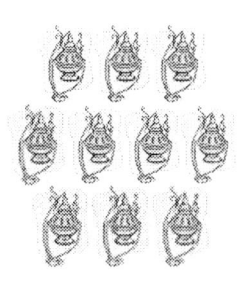

Will God love me more if I pray more?

"God loves us the way we are, but too much to leave us that way"
~ Leighton Ford

God has demonstrated enduring, unconditional love for us clearly in the Passion, death, and Resurrection of our Lord and Savior, Jesus Christ. If we need reassurance of the infinite depth of God's love you need only read and reflect the Passion account in one or more of the Gospels.

Can you – can anyone – love all of humanity and each individual person a fraction as much as Jesus demonstrated love? Ponder that thought as you reflect on the Passion of Christ.

Once you resolve your doubt, once the Passion account sinks deeply into your soul, consider again whether more prayer on your account can possibly increase the depth of God's love for you.

With the same scripture, sit in God's presence and reflect. If you have needs (and who does not have needs?), would God not know them and care about them and love you less if you prayed more briefly? Going farther, would God love you less if you prayed not at all, but simply presented yourself in all your love and all your pain and all your need at the foot of the cross?

Consider the gospel account of Jesus raising the dead son of the widow of Nain (Luke 7:11-17). She neither voiced a request nor even, in any way, petitioned Jesus for help, but simply expressed her sorrow in tears. Jesus, "moved with pity" (Luke 7:13), raised her son from death.

Because God is Love, God wants to love us beyond all measure.

Consider the gospel account of the man born blind (John 9:1-41). Again, the man neither asks for healing nor presents himself to Jesus for help. Jesus, however, acts to heal the man because, as He says, "While I am in the world, I am the light of the world." (John 9:5).

Because God is Love, God needs to love us beyond all measure.

"More" signifies a form of measure. Can we measure God's love? Love either exists or does not exist.

If Love does not exist, that is, we do not know or experience God's love, then we live in darkness and fear.

If Love does exist, that is, we experience and bask in God's love for us, then nothing we do or say can increase it, decrease it, or measure it. It simply envelops us, enriches us, and finally becomes part of us.

Having pondered whether praying more or less will alter the measure of God's love for us, take a moment to consider your prayer life and the love of God.

You pray as a means of walking with and being with God in your life. As you allow God into your life, you sense God's presence, God's love more. Not that God loves you more or less than God already loves you; rather, from your perspective, you make yourself available to the embrace of God's love for you.

In this way, the more you "pray always" (live lovingly), the more you realize God's love for you.

Ultimately,

We pray not
to convince God to act favorably
in response to our needs and wants;

We pray
that our needs and wants break open our minds
and hearts
in response to the will of God.

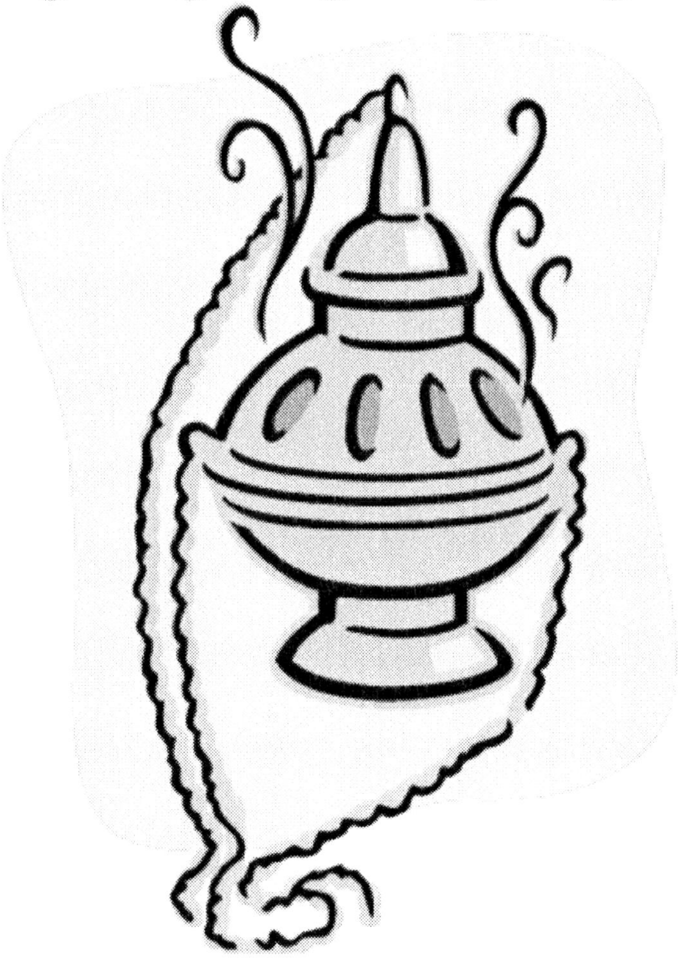